END OF EMPIRE

END OF EMPIRE

Marissa Davis

PENGUIN POETS

PENGUIN BOOKS
An imprint of Penguin Random House LLC
1745 Broadway, New York, NY 10019
penguinrandomhouse.com

Set in Minion Pro
Designed by Catherine Leonardo

LIBRARY OF CONGRESS CATALOGING-IN-PUBLICATION DATA
Names: Davis, Marissa, author.
Title: End of empire / Marissa Davis.
Description: [New York] : Penguin Poets, 2025. |
Identifiers: LCCN 2024051406 | ISBN 9780143138471 (paperback) |
ISBN 9780593512548 (ebook)
Subjects: LCGFT: Poetry.
Classification: LCC PS3604.A972555 E53 2025 |
DDC 811/.6—dc23/eng/20241209
LC record available at https://lccn.loc.gov/2024051406

Printed in the United States of America
1st Printing

The authorized representative in the EU for product safety and compliance is
Penguin Random House Ireland, Morrison Chambers, 32 Nassau Street,
Dublin D02 YH68, Ireland, https://eu-contact.penguin.ie.

There appears to be a law that when creatures have reached the level of consciousness, as men have, they must become conscious of the creation; they must learn how they fit into it and what its needs are and what it requires of them, or else pay a terrible penalty.

—WENDELL BERRY, "A Native Hill"

So we are here in the weather, here in the singularity. Here there is disaster and possibility.

—CHRISTINA SHARPE, *In the Wake: On Blackness and Being*

Contents

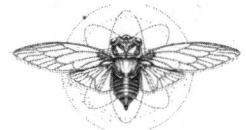

THE GOSPELS

GENESIS

END OF EMPIRE

Lot's Wife Triptych

a cold spring—an epiphany
bludgeoned—

threadbare, a land—without riotous irises—violet
to suture the whine of dust—

this country—a nacre slaughterhouse—
a plowed migration route, a dissonance

of grapevines—only my husband
would give the newcomers—a place to pose

weary heads—our neighbors, loyal to covenants
of use—what the generations—fungal, fruit, breaking—

all being down to colony—the seraphs,
archiving—mutagenic & catalyzed—now

a salvo of sulfur—clobbers the olive fields—ferrous
floods wolfing our streets—the sky fly-

hemorrhaged, greensick—a woozy
reckoning—

let me begin again—
I turned—I couldn't stop me—once, I was

a girl—& owlsong
hauled dusk—back to these woods'

black branches—& what of my children—
my arthritic mother—where else to go—on earth—

heartbreak—no—corrosion—was I
other—closer—than a brute

beast's whelp—avatar of my enemy—splitting
hazard's marble skin—& yet no python—

who could whip my shape
to shed it—

        let me begin again—
            I was stripped

        of country—by
            this country—this country

        pillaged—my name
            from my face—configured me—

        unnatural, apparatus,
            less soul than—flesh

        technology—convenient wed
            of yoke & ox—ground

        my father to dust—& robbed
            his harvest—chained my mother

        to her body—then trained her
            to banish it—this country

        target-practiced—anti-alchemized—
            bastardized

the love in me—salted crop—
    charred dahlia—what peculiar

triumph—to watch ruin—
    succumb to the ruin

it birthed—our twin threads whorling—
    one fray—

set—to snap—I was a rage—
    first, then clean

rapture—reborn heretic—hard
    as mineral—under

a xanthous moon—sloughed
    new—

REVELATIONS

Psalm for the Unloved Body

1 all we share is our hunger & we hunger for penance. so we pray for a banquet of stonings. so we pray to be thrown onto a pyre of battered lyres, 2 to incinerate beside ourselves, say for once we were together, in fact the last song left unbroken. 3 we have always been both bound & breaking—edenless where gaze makes either gagged angels or beasts of us. 4 what I mean is even now I am thirteen shaking on a street corner after a strange man says he wants to smell me. 5 even now I can't stop hearing *fat fat little nig ger girl who would ever want you* & screaming who said it who said it was it my whole good-soiled country was it me. 6 o my body, my little noose, my little split-yarn slipknot, how we sunder, if we sunder it is on ly to save us. each of us the red sea, each of us one hand of a weary prop het. we cleave homeland from homeland, we rift valley, we sift through the land's fingers, I become untouchable 7 & to thank you I write *lo ve love love love love* on your palms 8 until the word becomes only a gut string's numb staccato. now it means nothing 9 & can't be taken from us. now it means *body, could you ever be mine again? back to a little laugh-cheeked brown girl dancing naked in the summer rainstorms, mine?* now it is a tiny scythe you carry in your cheek & I pretend it doesn't scratch. 10 all we share is our hunger, so we pray for a harvest of blunt blades. so we pray to unswallow the skeleton key—to relock the errant titan's box or exhume its one buried benediction. 11 so we pray for a hailstorm of doves: that singing, that singing, such grace it's a cruelty, my voice almost recalling the way it felt to shelter in your mouth: not a blankness, 12 but truth stunning those hard muscles: & fire, & flight

Elegy for the Living

for the classmates of Tamir Rice

heard they
the willow
weep-
ing hard
salt & sev-
eral seas

the moon once
a smile now
a mad dog's long-
est tooth

warbles red
down rob-
ins' chests
pours red
from ev-
ery maple
in the blaz-
ing country

see they
april's gr-
in gone
crook-
ed ask what
good now
that bright-
sweet air

turned vis-
cous on
the skin

& what
will mean
the first-blo-
omed vio-
let now (vein-
blue) or the
clover (un-
braided &
paler than
hurt) or hop-
scotch squares
leap-empty or
the art of se-
cret hand-
shakes or any-
one's good name

where did
it go the un-
blistered free

era when
mamas at
least pre-
tended not
to pull shades
talked dusk
tigers prowl-
ing only late

late to papa
          you hear
                    that pop
          another
                    metal fang
          you see
                    the news

ripened they
quick by the
no-sun

& stopped
asking how
to spell *lav-*
ishly & *lum-*
inous or if *x*'s
in algebra want
to be found

instead
how many
pounds will
it be   life-

long that
locked le-
ad weight
of all
their pre-
tty

Dys/morphic Dis/order

both / the loc / usts

& the / once / -crop

mute / with loc / usts

ghazal refra /

cted in ice / water

elegy's au / bade

welp / ing sun / rise

in / to night / shades

a bru / te tong / ue shack / ling

eye to / *entro* / *py*

the so / und smo / ke makes

just be / fore / the temple

has cons / ented / to burn

the so / und / a how / ling

mo / uth makes / when it / makes

no / sound

is / wash / ing

rain / water down / the south / ern

bank with sna / ke's blood

is glass-sna / red

jaw / less

panic / king in

a / house of ang / els

vis / ion voo / doo / ed

into / ash

made sack / cloth

pan / theon waste / land

slit- / winged che / rub

fig fruit / & its mother- / wound

of wasp / egg

a / butterfly re / bounding

into the val / ley of de / ath

the eve / ning puzzle

day / light is / loath

to unta / ngle

an e / clipse misman / aged

co / ld split / ting tot / ality's

circ / umfer / ence whi / le

the / star / lings mur / mur

in a para / noid lang / uage

Antigone in the Bluegrass

still there

        & now each breath of me a bat

                still there

                        tearing

through the streets

             hoping to echo off

    McAtee's body was

                  his body

to find

                        where my brother

      amid days

                    was left

         for the new hard sun

            to blister, left

for the turkey vultures

                          rushing in heat

         from the western woods

                    & i am running towards water

                                                    still there

                                                           but where

                                          is the river & where

                        amid days

              are the gods

                                  of protest

        & why have they brought

                                  over violence

        us here

                      ignoring the virtue of night

    there is no such thing as

        law

               psalm

when my brother's heart lies

   slack

        in a garden of dust

                  McAtee had been

   no beds

killed

where our heads can rest

McAtee had been

no homes

for our weary nourishers

killed by law enforcement

i am tired of trying

to seek beauty

or shape it

over violence

or trust anything

that claims this empire

nation-

is worth more

than its own

wide

ash

yes i too can be

violence

bloodthirsty, clawing

for words that could strangle

a flag, bring a king

to my breast, leave him

laid in the streets

begging for milk

how i would dance when he starved

McAtee had been killed by law enforcement

all my skin

on fire, all my blood

wailing & my lungs

so many aftershocks

McAtee's body was still there

i have for impossible centuries

hunted for the river's edge

in Louisville, Kentucky

through smoke, but tell my brother

protesters gathered

fear unravels its dominion

tugged down by the moon of his name

in his name

we scrape off their gospels of

midnight

violence

drought & will give him

to the tender dark waters

ourselves if there is no law

that will bless

McAtee's body

his burial, no god

still

listening

for the sweet

of our family's pulses

nor to the war drums ringing

there

in that gap

o come my cousins

gather

let us batter their altars

Notes Left for the Ohio River to Read After It Tells Me It Has Forgotten Its Source

it begins with the damming
obstacle. or desire's indecipherable
hieroglyphs. or tide hoarse as a spirit
shouting back to its body
from a misremembered bank.

—

you flood & forget the fish
once sour april sheathes its storms,

let high noon bind
their bodies to pavement.

how can i trust you
to dredge for the elegant bones?

—

i ask your name
& your tongue schisms

      : intentional mistranslation of life
into market calculation. history, a pageant
of abattoirs. profit, a conspiracy
of pillaged children

      : rebirths unwound
from kinetic mud & shadow; chance
of a mouth to prod dangerous language:
        my self my self my self

—

i speak my name back:

cold-boned thankless.
girl south-born

but wearing her own skin,
& then wearing her body

out of it. split, as water
from bank:

at birth
i was blessed with a self

& in life
i laid waste to it.

whatever fool beast
starves

on purpose. echo
invoking an invented

division,
straining

to free the body
of the body

where the body
was free.

—

(imagine: knowing the self flood & not the flood-
ravaged house it was named,

& vanquishing current, & outwitting omniscient
cottonmouth, & wagering breath to flow towards it—)

—

if the source were stone,
whose virtue is to know its own
before, & be it, & be absolved by it

if the source were wound
scarred whole, balmed
with christening.

—

we practice:

river, spelled:
tides that still to listen
when the blackbirds sing

woman, spelled:
bronzeskin the sun
nuzzles scorchless bright,
hair a black nimbus

river, spelled:
autumn waters spilled
to feed the sunspun corn

woman, spelled:
i breathe. i breathe. i breathe.
& something flows
feverish in me

river, spelled:
blue seam, blue
annunciation, vein
anarchic, vaulting

towards the sleeping fault line,

—

where rock,
too long weighted

with false name,
will crack

a continent's bones
to rebuild.

Ecclesiastes: Deciduous

come winter, our permutation: canopies of capillary.
       shelter of sturdy bronchiole.

                our vegetal
          articulating animal. suggestion

of revelation. who can say
     which side is mirror. girl, recall
your name. night takes

          nothing. yields.
        bare alchemy
        of rest. below
       the asphalt: our roots
        work mutely
       in such radical slow

it would break you.
     in winter, you want

           to croon *mother*, you want to play viceroy,
         forget judgment, forget hunger, melt into something
          thicker than thought, become a being
        that could forget its skin, too,

unexplain the manufacturing of self,
     pull flesh back like orange peel—

       divulge the jubilee of tributaries, rouge throb, the you
     designating you, circle before it is inscribed as circle,

live tension
              between ink
& blank. our leaves drip
              into a syntax
of surrender—gild

                                        rubbling to brown,
                              becoming, with sunstretch,
                                    renewal's muscle—

              & the remainder
        wants nothing
              but its own elements.

What would I be,
        if I, too, could be this?—

                        even your question,
              a kind of symptom.

Demeter & Child

a poem in two voices

<u>Demeter</u>

<u>Persephone</u>
mama always saw the arriving hand
that noose of fingers   twining ankle

saw that something in her cracked
like the face of a watch
& the fog,

the fog
in my gaze   trellising
then i knew
she could smell hell on me

when she asked,

what if the heart's only a worn-down waterspout
the body a shineless dagger?

I took
a marker to the glass—
you are lovely, you are loved,
you are brilliant, you are kind—knowing

there are things a daughter might learn
that are worse than sex; knowing

the many mouths that awaited her; the serpents couched
in chrysanthemum fields: how she would ache
to mimic floret—moony, frail, the body

she thought other bodies
would want to hunt & gather,

& if i asked

what if the body's only an overripe fruit
the heart a flaying rope?

there they were: the traces of it, settled on her
like a net, like yellow smoke, shade of stars
all pulverized & matted—

                                        (imagine   seeing a being
                                                in the mirror
                                                just askew
                                            of who you are
                                            the difference
                                            only the size
                                    of a hair   but the size
                                        of a hair the size
                                            of a rift valley

                                        & then it possesses

                            all their gazes   shaping you
                    vaguely more monstrous each time
                                more monstrous or simply
                    not existing   how long before this
                            would make you too a reel
                            of unforgiving seasons—)

so I'd warm the milk.
draw the bath. grain by grain,
pick the pale sand
out of her coils. scrub her
till my palms rawed, till they
split & seeped,

                                        pinking my bathwater

though still it glinted off her—

                                        not the hunger i could not jettison

but her refusal
to speak to it—so it returned,
of course, that keening,

                                        the sound of gray
                                    hissing from the floorboards

                                              i couldn't stop
                                                    fainting

                                          & my eyes were not
                        my eyes   there was nothing outward
                    stepping in them anymore   my breath

                            was not my breath   but a tide
                                              of lazy mercury

                                              & when i asked

                what if the heart's only a dug-out land
                    the body a rusted shovel?

                                            she knew i'd gone
                                            back down again
                                    what i'd eaten   so little
                                            so   so little

of her could be left
unlocked. we'd have to make tradition

                                              of my plunging in & out
                                                of hellfire   where i
                                                slept all day   where i
                                            gnashed my hands   where i
                                                pummeled myself pulpy
                                                    in my sleep   where i
                                        was mostly timelessness & salt

                                                    some years love meant

orbiting in each other's guilt.
a labored kindness, how she played pretend:
come up briefly, suck the bruises, delay
the asking:

                    what if the body is only a smothered furnace
                            the heart the slimmest of rockslides?

                                                    i'd tried   but
                                    i was bloody-knuckled again   i was
                                        chomp-tongued   i was hollow
                            -eyed & shaking   i'd been up all night
                                                    smacking mirrors

what could I do
once she ran to the yard,
half-swallowed dirt, but spit it out,

once she hacked
down the garden's fruit, & smashed them,
left their splayed skins for the sun to punch,
then spelled her name out on the browning grass
in chewed-up arils

                              (the name
I closed my eyes & wove for her, offered her
beside my body's bouquet of blood & milk,
when she was only lung, hunger, my comfortable faith
in all the good she'd be,

her round nose, lips
like mine, then hardly the size of a thumbnail,
which I built in me, like all of her,
painstakingly, as we amplified

together in a paradise
of cells—I'd never felt
so humbled by anything:
slow patternings, her wrists, her legs, her eyelashes
as minute as the fur of a tomato stem—then, within me,
as now, outside, sublime kaleidoscope
of her becoming self—how
did she forget—)

what could I do

                                        but watch me plummet & tear
                                         her hair & rage   sacrifice
                                      the good china to the kitchen
                                            walls   the walls ate
                                             sheen sheek sheen
                                                    all night

                                              while i ground
                                           my teeth   howled
                                              into the pillow

                                        all the hounds all the bleak rivers
                                              webbing through us

I couldn't stop
losing her

& hurling cold & slicing
open sky till its hazy meat showed

& roaming the barren earth
prostrate praying
she might learn to catch herself

                                        i tried   i swear   i tried

by year's end
was there any skin left on my knees

                                        i do love her:

                                                        that
                                                      the leaf

                                              clung to the ice-
                                                  numbed tree

                                              the matchstick
                                                  shallowing

                                                    a solstice
                                                      cold

                                                        but

always hell back
scratching at her.
always that misted
gaze. always a fetish
for the hollowed
stump, for the crater left
where a lake has dried.
always an orphean glance back
into empty. scissored dance
to match it. always
priestess of her own
decrescendo. always
hell back & snaking
up her throat

& when she asked me,

     what if the heart lacks a zenith mama what if the body's
   only a rogue match in a zeppelin
    what if the body is elision what if the body is always too much mama mama
what if the heart is a broke-down wing
     what if the heart is feathering but the feathers
        are bent-tipped sewing needles what if the body
      is the sound of its own breaking what if
    the heart's that feeling when you cross a high bridge & realize
  that it might happen that the world could ripple just then & all of a sudden
     you'd be falling down down & the river
      that once seemed only vapor
   now you've been taken by it swift
    like a kidnapping—

came winter.
the earth clamorous

with wind. the earth
dusted white as
grief. all I could do
was hold
the hope of her,
begging:

what if the heart is
only you, what if the body is only you, what if you
are just one more of many forests being razed?

JUDGES

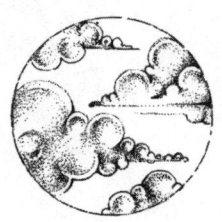

Ecclesiastes: Storm

i.

                              blue bud

                                                  of calamity,

we. leak

                              of hot iron, we.

                  water as

                                        creation & water

as collapse—

                        devourer

                                          of limestone,

                  earthbreast

& shelter. o mother,

                        we, o lunatic

                                                rot, o unbearable music

                  of touch, o hurt, o harps

made of leaves' backs,

                    o voice as immutable

          reign. o we,

                                        a violence remembering

              that in the beginning

any word could be named

                                a conjugation

            of love. we

                                            are everything's

destiny: indivisible,

                                    the rehashed caverns

              from the scattering

                        of seedlings from the coastlines'

illustration from the felling

                of the elder trees,

                                        their epiphanies of root.

we, the knot,

                    the tiers, the barren

                    slate, the switch-

                                        blade beguiling

                                                            void

ii.

            with grace,
we would have said. but on its belly
            crawls a novel world. there are children
of adam & there are children
            of eve & there are children
of only the tree, which bore fruit whose color
            was a libation, like a pouring of blood that in falling
caught voice & could sing the name of God,
            that tree which more than anything else
had God in it. & that was the danger:
            not that the elements would mix,
but that only one knew its nature,
            so that the others under the black weight
of this knowledge would have to labor
            to become it, & if they couldn't,
then consent to break.

            & they couldn't.
& thus began the age of appetite.
            the injustice is that we are altered, too,
in the unsheltering: the songbirds
            have also learned to fear us, & the waters
are given more than their memories can bear, we mean
            we give them more, we
torment. an accident.

we swear. we never asked to be the hammer
slow-forged by a trial of human hands.

      in this realm where each part comprehends
its purpose & relation, there is no true sin

      but division, but to subvert the primeval
balance, & there is no hell

      but to watch the self becoming
a sudden nucleus of crisis:

      we once were a shifter of worlds,
merely that, even in our occasional anger,

      & now, what comes from us?
there is the tower.

      there is the lightning lashing
like a thousand dissonant tongues.

Twister Tristate

Kentucky, Illinois, Missouri: November 2005

Wind, just
wind. Simple

as the possibility
of death. We slouched away

as taught: crouching over bone-
blue carpet, child hands

prayer-laced over
our necks—peach-soft

part of us, still silk
from birth. Our fingers

still new cartilage. Our mothers
far from us. Jesus

wept, & all the little children
in the school hall as teachers

rearranged our hands' formations.
Around us, heaven

a tight muscle: popping
like mamaws' knees.

None of us knew, no one knew
then, we had been born

too near the end of days.
All that ageless sky gone smart

as a crow, incandescent
with long memory:

done watching
the generations

throw different shapes
of stone & smoke,

hard smother, for centuries.
In this, so close

to coal country,
old powerhouse heart

of a nation brazen
with waste, that sky

would look at us
& know

what we had come from,
what our hands had taken

& other hands would take—
& revenge

the reap, the ripping.
The delta's torment

hardly a season
from our backs,

we could trace exactly
what we'd been spared—

how nimbly water
amplifies, beats wind

rabid. & we could see
the barbed fate arcing

towards us, what horizon
held, opaquely,

for those like us—
we, mostly, just the poor,

the poor's children,
once & future

laborers, quick-forgotten,
a little world

of little messengers
poised to be

left lead-chested.

If we had known,

someone would have said to buy kerosene.
someone would have said: *fell the trees, if only the ancients,* or

the birds, they have gone oddly still, hardly breathing
in those branches clean as the bones on a glutton's plate

or asked, *what on earth do the bats want, crying like that, & why*
is every small life fleeing.

mother, knowing such long stillness is a kind of vertigo,
would have made us all pray our travelers' mercies

& father, raised by women, would have spared
the hillside's elder crab apple, guessed we wouldn't perish for it.

if we in the town had been called out our doors by some autumn prophet,
she would have warned us—

come year's break, watch for crystal. watch for stars to spatter in the distance,
for sky to recover such immaculate black

it will make you clean as birth:
the stars which would not be stars, but transformers bursting—

brief contagion of fireworks blueing the low horizon,
flashing down to barrenness. the barrenness: what remained. like a pharaoh

somewhere had talked his way into a grave mistake: first beauty, fugitive, then the pines
falling everywhere,

common as the skins of a future summer's cicadas, as the mysteries
that claw out of clouds' bellies like another world's spawn.

& that gleam, that weight, implausible. the sycamores opaled & shimmered &
cracked & plunged & the oak branches swayed & stung the power lines

& the maples, ice-mauled, threw fatal shapes on the county roads, islanded Benton from
    Reidland,
Paducah from Possum Trot, Lone Oak from atomic Ballard, every family from every other
    family,

forcing us close to our visible breath, to dark & water—something like a womb
but treacherous; less transparent than the beast of summer,

which we did know, every year, would have us, in yellow mania, twining drought & flood.
but in this—our tender southern winter—we had believed

home something more solid than a warbler's nest.
harder fight for clouds' whim. some days one knows while living them

were already written in apocryphal gospels. so close to diamond, that judgment
warping over the branches of the birch trees, of magnolias

restless for martyrdom. metamorphosis of world into glass,
& our reflections grew dense & lucid in us; glass into vengeance,

& we noted, then, the purpose, a first expression
of something unnameable—unnameable, but solid, yes, so tangible

it could crack us all like a twig in its hand.

Spring in the Key of Pyrocene

June 2023, after the wildfires

Taciturn, this reddened heaven, its mask of earth.

        June's proclamations keep mum, approaching igneous. Iron

as frustration of ambient noise. A season of migration

        is regular spellwork, magnets toiling like ants in the soil. But this?

A wind bewitched. Our city is mauled. If orange unshelters,

        what to say of its provenance? O blackbird wing, o rupture

of temperature, o Cassandra whose mouth is rancor

        made sepia sun: *Even your bodies will grieve.* Our lungs,

smote by funeral, concede. Across a fiction called border, a sublimation

        of sublimity; a carnage ripe

to roam, dehiscent as the pods of impatiens.

        The solid centuries incinerate, vanish

into dust. & rage to challenge us.

Parable for the Apocalypse We Built, I:
The Forum

after Cavafy

What is it? What is its name?

> black widow. beech tree. the snake that was the staff of moses.

Will it survive?

> we do not know.

Will we survive?

> we will not survive.

Did this era birth no prophets?

> one lacked all shape
> but two hands: a fist
> of wind, a fist of rain.
>
> season by season,
> each smote us. & still
> we did not retreat.

What is it? What is its name?

> manta ray. swallowtail. basalt. lactobacillus. creek.

Will we survive?

      we will not survive.

Will it survive?

      we believed that it would perish,
      yet still, if changed, it lives.

Are we the thing that *evil* means?

      no. yes. no.
      our faces, combined, form a prism of holes.

Will we survive?

      we will not survive.

Will our children survive?

      a percentage of pattern we share with the fruit bats;
      of our elements, with limestone.

What is it? What is its name?

      wildebeest. a plague of locusts. salt. our hungering lungs.

How can it survive, if dying?

      its nature is to alter.

How can it survive, if dying?

      its nature is to see no part as separate.

How can it survive, if dying?

      its nature—

Did we not deserve a prophet to warn us?

      having no teeth, no tongue, fungi
      graced the roots of trees
      with language.

      over several summers,

      we burnt them alive.

Parable for the Apocalypse We Built, II:
Doe of the Haruspex

i   a wound & ascent

i   motion made relic

my   liver quaking   fat as era in your palm

        guts a pit where light pounces & withers

you   carve my ochre-haired layers

        unsecret my elegant vein

        with nails a clot of thunder you un-

           ravel me rearrange me to

sketch birthblow lovefall emperors' chance

        your flesh on my flesh your knuckles

a curse   even in sameness

you   make my body

        technology take my body

to use   in wasting   brother

        what else can i give to you   you

so unlike   the anxious vipers

        the wolves   that nuzzled

the softness   pinking my sisters' throats

        until they slept deeply   in the deep of them

even the worms would make me

something   greater than myself   seeing i

        too mothered wilderness & future

now the slit through my core gapes   to a margin

        between worlds   age plucked from age

all of me

        spilling   all of me

          screaming organ

halt & stagger   every nerve of me

        burning with

           end

small consequence

of your steadfast misery

your   need & questing &   want & want & want

ask any question   to my gelling blood

      the beast of me   will spill

one answer:

my   ruin

is   your

ruin   my ruin

is your   ruin my   pomegranate

      heart's last push is yours

what triumph   of the blade

      in your sturdy fist

now brother   come close

      your eyes with me

    let us remember once more

how the thrushes' songs

   used to

            light our

   brief backs

           like

                 sunflare

Wild Grasses

      as a girl, bare legs ablaze
with pollen, tamed beasts would pull you
into the wild grasses—

                        across the torch of midday,
              august's illegible twist & cut. roar
                  of those tall unnameable flowers

& pond frogs, field mice,
        wasps & yellow jackets, hornets,
               & whatever force teased them upward, outward.

                                 fear was not knowing a face
                                    until it struck.

no warning, though sometimes
the dog would balk, its leash yank

                           your sun-damp hands, before something split
                  the wave grass,

some angular primordial face,

          if not toad
        then snake,
          if not black
        then corn,
          then one

                of those awful kinds
                        with death wetting their mouths—

their lips a fulcrum
between equinox
      & annihilation, a known world
left swaying at the skin's edge.

     & you'd grow strange, then—consequence
of such a minuscule mouth,

                     filament of fang,
                        half dew-drip of venom—

     made birth-slick, hound-
eared, deer-gazed, girl
       resharpening the wan dulled animal.

       & you'd feel, unsealing, a different possible.
       first, an impact

     dense as conviction, blunt force
like an arrow running

            neat through bone. then, a poison's
             eloquence: you, unwinding,

   unyours. toppled.
     down & down,
       back into the land's
         carnival of root,

    where the long red worms, the patient
      hyphae, would derange
your architecture, repattern you.
      & you'd belong again.

now, here, tall-grown, you roam
the famed gardens
of a skeletal city.
the sky is muzzled
with concrete.
your woman-feet
pad the sand-paths,
carelessly skirting
all this flora
combed & pearled
into *allée* after *allée* after *allée*—
    & your eyes are searching—

        still, still—

among clean lanes
of indexed flowers—

        for what those wild grasses hid:

    summer's legion of oblivion jaws,
creatures beyond the rim of utterance,
      beyond negotiation—

      & roamed too close, you would know
      whose dominion. you would know your place.

Ecclesiastes: Thirteen-Year Cicada

our selves less self
than a knowledge

of time. time:
our shell, our salt,

our singing wings.
our wings like flakes

of mica, pining.
the land

splits its skin open
to free us,

& again, to lay us
down to rest.

systole. diastole. in all
directions: imminence,

the land emitting
a smell like love.

in the flash
between beats—

the still
of wholeness. summer,

we ate
& fucked & ate.

day a unit
to measure want.

want inseparable
from need.

deathless, we bury
our bodies' present;

our bodies' future
wearing the shell

of another body.
the land names us

synapse, & we are
memory, waiting

to crack
its border.

there is no border.

THE GOSPELS

Thirteen Ways of Looking at a Dead Fish

East Palestine, Ohio

there is no available canary however the yellow
scream of a fox that has splintered its legs
trying to outrun its own end may suffice

—

one could almost believe the old dog simply ambled
into the light of the waxing gibbous

that daybreak would not disclose his shell
rigid as glass in the violent dew

—

forty years my grandpa worked
Ohio railroads iron tree branching
from southern hollers sending coal sap
stout as moonshine to sweeten glutton
tongues of the near north's factories

in his foothill town we can't
drink water from the tap
without sickening, we shower quick
before blighted with inexplicable rash

it has been this way so long
we don't ask questions

—

daddy just home from
the industrial glue factory peels
Calvert chemicals off his fingers,
clicks his tongue,
sighs *vinyl chloride?—*
that's some toxic shit

mama says she's just glad they'd had us
before he was ever made to touch it

—

not a hen in the county
whose eyes would catch the peony
smear of another mountain daybreak

a legion of spotted bass belly up in Leslie Run

—

The fish yes
there was an impact to those. However—

—

Schrödinger's cat of my mother's
maybe-cancer. practically
untestable, the ovaries that mapped
the half of me, child to uncage
at the foot of a floodwall mural proclaiming
Welcome to the Atomic City

fist of this tyrant kingdom: my city
of industry, my city of atom bomb,

my city of warheads, of plutonium kept
clandestine, of slow killings
accomplished to more efficiently
kill, of truths & metals
forced underground

I know where the river runs
& looking odds in the eye will break me

—

someone somewhere is always dying
& someone somewhere else pays a mortgage
with their finishing breath

now over a state line, now over a border

—

another business model another cost-cut
another behemoth on a flimsy track
another layoff another shift another shift
another layoff another consultant
another cost-cut another hedge fund
another business model another acronym
another euphemism another denial
of appropriate protections another cost-cut
another layoff another business model another
acronym another shift another shareholder another AI
without oversight another bottom line another
euphemism another axle bent to breaking another behemoth
on a flimsy track another accident another
accident another accident another accident
another poison found in the river that raised us

—

Opened in

       an impoverished region

trainloads

       uranium

for bombs

       exposure

into the 1990s

       by then

plutonium

       permeated

the land

       fishing ponds

campgrounds

       the community

has no idea

       "I was told

this is Paducah—

it doesn't matter here"

—

We all know how these stories go.

—

norfolk southern numbers games:

one-fifth—of jobs cut in the last

five—years, the slide to understaffing, precisely scheduled, to reap

fifty-billion—dollar valuation, for company railroading on a brake system

one hundred fifty—years old, battling courts against upgrades that could dent
their

fifty-billion—valuation, ensuring the environmental disaster of nearly

fifty—cars derailed or damaged,

eleven—of which contained highly hazardous substances, prompting the company
with a

fifty-billion—valuation to offer as damages to the city

five—american dollars per chronically endangered inhabitant

—

[an impact][a conflagration][a migraine]

[an understanding within our nerves][a weeping

in the creeks][a sinking salamander][an evacuation zone]

[a rigor mortis][a gradual massacre][a dog

dead under moonlight][a patient

consequence][consequences][a seeping

into the earth][of us, our animal]

[bodies, our delicate cells][their chorus,

discordant][disquiet in our][queasy guts, our groundwater]

[if there is nothing][that could harm us][why

are our arms][newly blistered][why][are our throats]

[too torn][to speak] yes   there was an impact

However—

Illuvium Archive

Recall: a swallowed decade, late morning: sky white as corrosion:
        an assault ambling over the threshold: the ice storm:

        was *a trauma*, sister says: we all pretend she's joking: we were only girls:
what fickleness: what arcane arithmetic of *gotcha: gotcha back*: an angered earth:

shifts paradigms: things used to be simpler:
        down in the valley, our mother sold corn silk to her classmates

        by saying they could smoke it: there wasn't google then:
& countries might agree ozone more significant

than dividends: extinction not quite yet brought
        to auction: a low island shudders: the guinea pig:

        froze to death that week, when our home was a lightless icebox:
sister refuses to remember: to dub a rodent

a millennial prophecy: we eldest are always tasked with the burden
        of right memory: tightroping protection, preparation:

        elusive: the equilibrium: a loss
of innocence: is learning with what swift simplicity a storm

might slaughter: holding in hopeful palms
        what refuses breath: a moment a child must will into oblivion

        to carry on: what we will into oblivion to carry on:
what becomes, in time, oblivion:

it all began so small:
        (if you can say this, you are lucky): in a future

that is now our past: a woman is driving towards the inundated east:
bringing fresh water. flashlights. to her mother: an embroidery

of vertigo: mist threading through thrashed mountains: our west
        had already been bewildered: the bluestem kneeling

        before twisters slipped from their untidy season
like blood from a cut: like *lama sabachthani*

from a mouth stunned by its own nearness
        to oblivion: though it was told.

Broke-Down Litany for an Empire's End

there are many small apocalypses,
an emergent complexity
like neurons' reticulum
or a colony of fire ants

disaster is always hypothetical
until it comes cat-scratching, fevers;
until it crosses the house's threshold
like a skeleton bride

horizon shape-shifts in the days of western blaze;
bent with anoxia, dawn forgets itself to sunset

if a bee is dying in a yard in West Virginia,
a bee is dying on a sidewalk in Beirut
if a bee is dying in an Alsatian creek,
a bee is dying on the small quakes of the Mekong River

one apocalypse is water,
one is the warmth that swells it

one apocalypse is that when a levee cracks
the brownblack towns drown first

this much light unnerves me,
a signature forged
in a smith's flame

how to account for the godweight of a hyphen,
trickster king that links & snaps?

the souls of pride & shame
have been bodyswitched

touch blade to the abscess
leaking antithetical

birthrights: an absence
or a surplus of heat

who will answer for $140 a head in Adelanto

one apocalypse was spit from the wooden wombs
of ships docking in Liverpool, in Nantes

my home-ripped foremothers have named
this time a sweet-mouthed strawberry
fracture. exactly what has been deserved. didn't curse it so
but laughed the wound open to pus, calling
let their bloodwalls crumble, barnyards wrath,
cotton rot or rage the plains.
they named us nothing.

i crawled into a rebeccan force,
gummed its clothes to my skin
like a coven of wood ticks.
coaxed to leap, to fragment myself
against the septic stones—
i almost did it.

if one apocalypse is islands' interment,
another is continents' nonchalance

if a bee is dying in the wire shadow of a burnt-bare redwood,
a bee is dying in a schoolyard in Addis Ababa

by a child's skinned knee.
a mingling of bloods.

today, Kabul falls
like a Kabul that is falling.
there are no similes
for the swallowing
of homes.

I consider the ancestors:
in the time-deep fields
of Carolina, stolen to toil
on a stolen earth, to nourish,
for centuries, someone else's spectral
abundance—their acrobatic
ability to steal.

cousins, we have wounds gagged quiet.
the cloth, like the wound,
is someone's precise, purposeful labor.

one apocalypse tunnels down a birth canal
shaped like a drone's steel guts

one problem being that *land*, in a devil's tongue,
translates so easily to *mammon*. a curse of assonance.

     & no one will be free until the land is free

       o language, i've nearly caught you. i see you close enough to spin a web.

     the hyphen's latter linkage is its own chopped syntax
     frankensteined to serve a border's grammar

       (which, in this context, means an utterance
       taking three dimensions, becoming porous

       in one direction—like a sphincter or the mouth
       of a sphinx, & thus, historically, a strangulation;

       a frontier or a furnace depending
       on where one's feet touch ground,

       where, on the paper edge of a rock's boiling core,
       one's mother yelled & broke into water)

i didn't send the missile, but
my gas sure was cheap.

       a bee dying in the track of a vanished river in Arizona
       a bee dying in a grave of sticks, once a Moroccan orchard

a bee dying among the should-be apples
a bee dying among the should-be oranges,
   hard little sunsets that would have tasted like
a bee dying among the whimpering basil buds,
among the quaking clockface heads of passionflower,
  counting down to

          the test results say oil
          is the father of at least 8.5
          apocalypses

who will answer for the children of Fort Bliss
who will answer for the lost women of Juárez
who will answer for the fathers of Darfur

who will answer for the breath of George & the breath of Philando
for what the ears of Gianna heard
for what the eyes of Dae'Anna saw

    honorable senator, what a timely investment in body bags

empire from proto-indo-european
pere: to procure. or it could have been *pere*:
to produce. or play around & drop
the bogus binary: we could speak

of what is procured for production.
the means to the ends, guaranteed
to be justified. the end, deemed justified,
rouges its damage *collateral*, dabs the wet lip
& makes a pretty face.

American sonata:
leave the past to the past.

if a bee is dying, it is dying
in the soundless, monumental way of certain saints

who will answer for it

when a headline blares: *Is this the fall of America?*
it can only be understood one way or the other.
if the first: daybreak is a program
scripted to malfunction. ready a dance

for the waiting graves of bullets
once betrothed to you,
condemned to die virginal—

—if the second: o enemy,
was there ever another choice? look
at this ruin, barbing backward & backward;
how each root bleaches the soil it grips.
this coffin was built when the cradle was,
& from that cradle's poison oak

flavor profile of an apocalypse, for once,
well-earned: sweetburn
of a hacked-open beehive; scar tissue
thickening a rose's red; coyotes'
water hymns, a blue balm
on the bloody valley; dusk
leaking down the left wing
of a swallowtail

                                   & so undoing becomes its own augury

call synonym the asymptote, plot
luxe & decay—the difference
tapering like daylight

                     our Manderley,

                     asphyxiating, our god-
                     damned house of damnation:

                     in a springless world,
                     this little kingdom
                     is deciduous.

                     rejoice. it's a kind
                     of justice. an oblivion
                     season burrows right
                     through our names.

For Columbia

Strange spring. Monday, we farewell, fenced by not a peace, not quite
an occupation. A condition we have no name for. White, the heat
flung from the copter's wings, the derangement of that cyclops eye,
prowling the campus all class. The sirens trawling Broadway,
hounds hardly in abeyance.
                          & the plummeting
mock orange petals, trying to mend this rupture in the air,
are white, too—such a white that only comes from bearing witness
to an elegy or psychotic break. When all is said & done,
someone will talk again of amendments, how free or not the tongue, the body's location,
on this robbed & inelegant soil. Simpler story. Who will speak of
                          the white of shrouds,
kaffans molding to narrow forms, marking stolen landscapes:
brow & nose, child lips that will be the lips of a child,
always. Cities & cities of plundered untils. Ships cracking in two,
the souls of their mothers: their grief-beyond-grief, blank
as the end point of language, as the end of the shore of time, where meaning stuns & buckles,
clutches all approaching light, & flees.
                          Spring of memorials, spring of barricades,
of struggle like spring, born south & wildfired
latitudes. Pink fever hell-bent on returning green its green. Feudalisms, overripe,
earthquake beneath your feet: you who returned our scraped-out heart its muscle.
Learned by heart the martyred poet's lines. You disobediences of mercies, incantations to
     unbury faith:
emperors' bright phobias & plagues upon hedonic parliaments. & all while knowing
no power will permit its own slippage, knowing the dogs chew the leash, knowing
                          Tuesday will be pandemonium
by dusk. Waning gibbous hauls blue tides, blue tigers, fire
tethered madly to the hand. Fingers emboldened by lightlessness. Any witness
has been forcibly removed. If padlocks beleaguer perjured gates, *invasion*
is the hour's word. In Harlem. In Rafah, exponential. In Harlem, in Rafah, the invaders

have broken rotten bread on rotten tables, polished one another's weaponry, assembled

a spring of terror, spring of nightsticks. How

is it the time of cherry blossoms, & any color on the concrete

is blood. These perversions of empathies. These manic & terrified judges. & gas, & pin, &

thrash of a body

besieged by electric current. Whose child is limp

at the foot of the great hall's steps. Whose child is battered on the ground.

Whose child is calling for the ambulance, the ambulance denied.

O young ones, the iron hand has come,

as the iron hand always comes, in defense of might & money,

& what you have brought upon yourself, you have brought upon us all:

to reckon with fear. With the measure of the roots of our fear.

& decide against it. We have watched you. We have netted the airwaves

in our fingers, massed before the gate's hermetic metal. We have torn our voices for you,

you, our terrible

beauties, murmurers of tempest, gardening revolt like azaleas, you who brought this down

upon us:

a spring of rebellion, spring of unfettering, of courage & this shock of hope.

From the other side of the inflicted borders,

where your bodies wait, sparrow-slight, so vulnerable to the blows they will deny

before the day's sharp edge, we hear you open your planetary mouths

to song: an elegy for annihilation, a bare-handed break of apathy, footstep into the legacy

of truth-telling, crack traveling through the riot shield. Your song, the careful hammer.

Your song, the mass

of petals midnight wind shoulders towards us, incandescent in the fissured spring—

rectifying,

rectifying even as it falls.

Ecclesiastes: New Madrid Fault

patience.
I brace

                to sing. to break
                like a runaway. clap

like a vulture's wing.
call me your near-private

                apocalypse. your homeland
                errant. little bee sting

on a planet's hulk. single chord
to an orchestral catastrophe.

                last time, I knotted river up
                & snipped her like slim ribbon.

I worried moonwane
into a dark map to anoint Tecumseh.

                I witched the silt to boil, crushed
                quartz down to shallow lightning, crowned

myself an emergence in reverse. a widened
        rewinding. brute

                paradox, I
        challenge. make a baptist

                of gravity. crack stone
                        like an ice sheet. waft the occult

perfume of groundwater.
wring the fields to warp & fissure.

                              gape to a gospel
                                        of earth as a verbose blade an ambiguous mallet.

calyx for a cicatrix, I'd eat you with a mouth

                              of scar tissue. my breath a low candle

                                        for land's unforgetting. isn't remembering

a life's most essential art. thick trouble

                              & a yolk for grief. & some hard

                                        illumination. I recollect every force

that ripples through me. I know where it births

                              & what fine thing builds from it, how abyss

                                        is apotheosis, makes me unconquerable,

a sumptuous shout. I unsick, outrank

                              all season, democratize in reminding

                                        the unbiased breakability

of bone. if I

                    blink, a world

                                                    revolts, rives

            its known

                              order seam

                                          from seam. after

    me, no

                              epilogue. no

                                                      road out but

reconfiguring.

Black Girl Kintsugi

mama said she was scared i would jump off a bridge { *my body hears the crack* } sister said
    please pretend

      you hadn't thought about it { *of floodgates & rouses, arms itself with* } the cruelest thing

is the lightlessness inside our own heads { *rampage,* } proof: the photo books where

      my grandmother annihilated { *revelation.* } her own face with ink   like this i know i too

must be { *this, a holler hard enough* } a hidden sin { *to snap a net.* } there is a mirror

      in my eye & { *when the pillar of lightning rips,* } it howls like a gibbous moon

{ *it says, hallelujah praise the atmosphere's unburdening,* } i mean wolf { *says, may the best
    animal strike twice.* }

      i mean the coyotes are { *my body is* } never that far from the banks   where i come
        from this is

{ *a wet & sinewed vengeance,* } fact not metaphor   nobody taught me

      how to hate myself   but everybody   i was { *a conjugation of element,* } raised staring

at salvation { *a moon waxing* } from the river's wrong edge   i'm not blaming you

      but i am { *lion-eyed.* } a tongue was { *i am becoming* } mine & wandered sovereign

before it was { *a fresh cosmology:* } bored through with history's { *invisible serpents,* }

      square unbearable teeth   dear america   my face { *black current, red morning,* } marks the epicenter { *continental quake,* } of your unreckoned shame   but you've got me

well trained & i have { *a wildfire* } never wanted anything { *for a heartbeat.* } but to be

as beautiful as you { *when i smelled chain* } decked in your silver bars   & blunt knuckles

{ *the year's first flowers slithered, sprouted* } your flexible lexicon   spent four hundred
years reclassifying

monstrous { *teeth, & war-cried.* } any way it could include me   can i wonder then why
such misery

troubles my blood   why i must mother my own language { *my body is* } america

{ *a dangerous world. whatever shackles it* } answer me { *must perish.* } have you ever felt

{ *untethered &* } so ugly you wanted { *belonging* } for generations { *to nobody,* }
nothing

but water i mean { *i am* } a river in your lungs { *the most immediate of gods*

Union

you were only
        plucking hyacinth.

spring gnashing over you:
        an urgency, a greed,

wounded by new brightness,
        the sudden gore

of its own empty. this, the beginning
        of knowledge:

birth commanded your mother outward.
        her hands: blooded echoes

of the black land. her hands:
        obedience made flesh, life-lines

heavy-slung with tulip bulb.
        nearby: child-you, child-sitting, crisscrossed

across the unchild earth.
        you watched surrender

without seeing it.
        until   (—you were only,
                        you were only—)

you sniffed the flower. decided,
        rashly. mashed its skin into yours—

broken stems, assault of sticky milk.
        oil seeping, leaping,

sprouting fang, puncturing
        your plumsmall wrists. this: the destruction

of the body, annihilation
           of limit, disparate forces flowing

as one, or a singular force
        shaped disparately, promiscuity

of essence, substance; you could smell it in you, now:
        its blood, your blood, dissolving, rising, until

new, thick-breathed, you shuddered
        into your warm, divisible elements—

once oriole, once fungus:
        gold down, torn light, mycelium.

weren't you, right then, also
        tulip bulb, & the hard dirt holding it.

also persimmon. rotting also in the weeds.
        also frenzy. tangled

mercy. bull thistle
        razoring the wind. also

without lack, as earth,
        immune to ruin; being

that earth & the everything
        that rages through earth, knowing exactly

what it is, exactly
        what it is owed.

march, & the south air
        already deep as river. you awoke

burning in the belly of it: a small thing
        suspended in her own

without-beginning, without-end;
        & your mother, nearby, oblivious

to how loud you did not scream. your mother:
        close-lipped. eaten with toil.

something in her sirening:
        from the earth you can

own nothing,
        not even yourself—

perhaps it was the sweat her body leaked
        onto the peeling bulbs;

you saw it—
        something of her

flowing down,
        & born, & buried,

& already lashing
        upward with them.

GENESIS

Diaspora Poetica

this tongue,
      lacking

                colostrum,
                is only

                                capable of
                                  plosives.

these teeth:
      pounding stones

                around a
                stilted amputation.

                                muscle graft
                                    where once

was low
      pearl. who

                could say
                its shade

                                or sea. now,
                                    in my face,

only instrument
      the way

                hearse is
                an instrument.

                                        in the mouth,
                                                air

calls forth
        a congregation

                        of deserts.
                        no sound

                                        bears grace
                                                enough

to unfell the
        woods—the word

                        as given, less
                        god than saw blade.

                                        the word
                                                as given, handed

-down window
        shade, dictating

                        spillage
                        of shadow

                                        & light. blue
                                                sun drags

I from its own
        face. a legacy:

                        in bowed
                        reflection

                                        bloom shape
                                            shifts into

banshee mouth,
        hardly more

                        than a filter
                        for dusk. a hurt.

                                        deliverance
                                            demands

dizzying a myth
        this granite,

                        to believe beyond
                        renaming, collage

                                        an idiolect from
                                            the unclean

break of brute-forced
        morpheme.

                        even the genealogy
                        is destruction. sacrament

                                        of ruin: once *tear*,
                                            as with a talon—

tablet stone or calf
        skin, the papyrus

                        still wrecked
                        with gracious

                                        muck, earth
                                                bodies anchoring

alliance. to inscribe
            is to blade-

                        cut;
                        pulverize

                                                & blow into
                                                        dust, take

arm in
            matter's battle

                        of balance,
                        study the wing.

                                                good violence.
                                                        graphite shred,

shiver & sharding,
            & rivulets

                        of dissonance
                        might arc

                                                in the blood.
                                                        note, freshly,

the kingdom's
            cracks. now shovel.

Memory of Mammoth Cave, Provoked by a Pelvic Ultrasound

You'll hear three sounds
created by the blood rushing through the uterus.
The uterus is made of several muscles—
the blood moving through each gives a different music . . .

—

in the whitewashed office, instruments of unusual revelation.

the organ, translated, aimed to stain me; gleaned glossolalia from the waves.

low throbs of an amphibian throat or the methuselah creep of groundwater.

once, as a girl, i touched the dew of groundwater.

a wanton palimpsest, that labyrinth, which all birth imitates.

i bore witness: the way gypsum leaps from cave walls is a brightness like a sound.

& bright this black, attests its roots: *glow, gleam, absolute.*

i was a child. i trembled, realizing i had already lived.

the organ knows. the organ tells on itself—calls me a side effect of time, an accident.

small lives living separately as one. failure & shed. sex & red revival. minor frisson of
    apoptosis & the cells' slick gasping splits.

i bore witness: a primordial darkness, dense as the nerves' charge that originates all thought.

the descent less a mimicry of death than a vision of death bound to its opposite:

a serpent skinning.

i: plurality, an accidental. creature chording high & low kingdoms. a trinity roars sharp
    from my bloodwet gut.

louder than i was ever told, that cosmos of hidden rivers. i bore witness:

in the hollows, a jasper-black to make the head whirl, as consummate as God's passing back,

which i & under-earth commune with.

which exhales & is sentient.

Katabasis

Persephone recollects

In a dream: cold rains falling
in reverse out the autumn earth

I felt my body & my body was salt water

I helped a doe loose a fawn from itself,
branch its flesh, surrender
half its heaviness to sun & breath with a force
as hot & mute as lightning
but the child—I held it in my hands—
the child was stillborn

In a dream I touched my loneliness, I smelled it
it had the texture of unkempt wool, the scent of semen
& I decided to keep it

The land turned to dust under my feet.
I took off my sandals, tried
to teach myself to step with lightness, tried
to kiss the hurt from its stone face
but even my mouth was a kind of acid

Under earth, I braided my hair with lanolin,
let my coils riot like roots. I believed
my own end to be no cruelty. Every soul
learned winter's bite but me
& I was happy

        no no
I was not happy, I wanted to run

through the storm-soaked fields again
& see cold branches
standing naked as a man
& tell my mother I'm sorry
for our twinned sorrows

I wanted to shout my own name over & over—
for once, it felt like a strawberry on my tongue,
that firm & real—& I could taste
the memory of ambrosia
o god   it was there   it was mine again

see, death is a kind of longing
just as longing is a kind of death

I am learning to love myself a little better here
& that means knowing
what I deserved. I deserved something
much brighter than this

In a dream the history I am made of
is not the history I am made of.
I am neither a sin nor a series
of endings. As I won't be.
In that world, I never staggered under sour
bloodbeads of pomegranate—
maybe there is even no such thing—

so when I look in the mirror
all I see is my life
performing the very action of life

my face more than a face,
a consummation & a radicle
a nucleus, a wellspring

I never wanted to wake up
but the earth

taught me many things,
including the necessity of closing a parenthesis

including that it is possible
to survive one's own death,
though you must be altered

I could almost die
for wanting me

All this light. My blue heart
thrashes like a fish

Singularity

after Marie Howe

in the wordless beginning
iguana & myrrh
magma & reef   ghost moth
& the cordyceps tickling its nerves
& cedar & archipelago & anemone
dodo bird & cardinal waiting for its red
ocean salt & crude oil   now black
muck now most naive fumbling plankton
every egg clutched in the copycat soft
of me unwomaned unraced
unsexed   as the zealous virion
that would rage my uncle's blood
or the bacterium that will widow
your eldest daughter's eldest son
my uncle, her son   our mammoth sun
& her uncountable siblings   & dust mite & peat
apatosaurus & nile river
& maple green & nude & chill-blushed &
yeasty keratined bug-gutted i & you
spleen & femur seven-year refreshed
seven-year shedding & taking & being this dust
& my children & your children
& their children & the children
of the black bears & gladiolus & pink florida grapefruit
here not allied but the same   perpetual breath
held fast to each other as each other's own skin
cold-dormant & rotting & birthing & being born
in the olympus   of the smallest
possible once before once

The Living Soil

an intentional *Erosion* of homeland's denotation. to speak
of *Nature* in most contexts is to speak of soil stripped &
swindled, the ubiquity of colonial gluttony. ghettoization
an irony pitch as petroleum, an irony lived alongside
Decline in Health, Deterioration in Food, the immortal menace
of detonations. *The Problem*, bestial, begins with the western
lust for watchdogs. all it takes is a british signature to
station a state, sentinel at the oil field's door. know that ink
can offspring atrocity just as easily as art. i.e., human
animals. i.e., the law of the jungle. i.e., *The Law of Return*, its
linguistic parallelism to The Trail of Tears, The Partition of
India, The Effects of Empire on who is included in a word
like creation, which is also, always, a question of exclusion,
a syntax sculpted to heave hypoxia on a people standing
on golden ground. ever industrial, *The Programme* tends to
favor partition. ask sykes. or the subcontinent. it takes fine
french wine & treaties signed at the witching hour to
quench an imperial *Need for Control*, to pour concrete in the
foundations of catastrophe. *Practical First Steps* says empire,
as it funnels mortiferous funds, unforbids phosphorus,
prompts an exodus to egypt, dams the exits, damns the
earth, damns the terre's damnés to drinking sea. nothing
more than best endeavours to facilitate the achievement of
the ally's object: not merely *Fragmentation* but acquisition
with no aperture. *Pioneering and the Individual* manifest destiny.
To survive, we thwart the individual, apprentice ourselves
to *Soil Ecology*, emulate *Mycorrhizal Associations*: Palestine,
long familiar, taught my people the treatment for tear gas;
painted our dead on the transgression of their prison's wall.
we comprehend, from varied angles, what it means to be
felony-sentenced for breathing, we peoples without
nations, despised on the lands on which we were born. *In Search
of a Starting Point* we first bear one another's witness, name
every father martyred with my nation's emerald blessings,
by men trained by the occupier's guard. we note the *Wider*

Application of the same clawed tactics: checkpoints & jail cells, bloodhound machineries, canonization of barb & border. o peccant architect, hawking possession for the *Value of Skin*, beware: we prepare our *Mycorrhizal Responses*, span & speak for miles under earth, note what systems to decompose, re-compose, channel *The Complexity of Compost Action*, & will recombine the fogging toxic elements into *A New Light*. as the hegemons ally, blood brothers sworn at the altar of a mammon god, so must we before a *Revolution in Outlook* & in action, discipled to the *Fertility Stored in Vegetation*, our continuance as knitted as fungus & forest root. *The Common Factor*: each people's perennial desire for *Wholeness, The Case Outlined* & struggled for: a dignity immutable. yes, there will be sustenance & safety. our children flying kites in fine weather. & what will burn? nothing. a sumptuous sun.

Altar-mondialism

everywhere, our roots touch

everywhere roots touch, a just insurrection

could be

second coming as in: to be stained with, then elated by, exile

if only transfigured by the margins, imbued with fusion at the exterior, is it possible to
    wring a lucidity worth deeming dangerous

how to be dangerous to my nation—

an arrogantly unsecular entity. each fiscal year, it pries open its twilight mouth to bark out
    new shrines. ha, holy, ha, the hydro

carbon trinity. a slew of true believers warm their feet at the tilted hearth. the priests of
    bondage singing

        dissection! reflux! parapraxis!

spread-eagle for the slippage of crises! blood wrung from even afterbirth!

cruets of new world silver, withered chains of hoary coral. in the herald angel's throat, a
    thriving angina, a false spring retching anemic lilies

tubercular, my nation's inverse hymns, staccato intonement of advancing penumbra

ossuary of the masses—cirrhosis of any biome once stewarded—accumulation threaded into
postmodern fugue—

aperture & limitation. union & fracture. many things can be true at once.
language   : stage actor cast in the role of border
                : an attempt to countervail the role of border   assumed by skin

i speak, you speak. we speak: true at once. articulation as joint.
conjugation a form of cartilage. mobile, the future perfect:

                    (

what will we have become ::

                    how will we have survived ::

who will have staunched our blood ::

                    whose blood will we have staunched ::

will any of the echoes we wring upon the world,
            a rain more desperate to conjure
shoot than any self-conscious April,
            have managed to matter ::

what will have been the impact of the lyric
            we imagined meteoric :
the role of property, of poverty, of poetry :

                    the *I*: a shovel to dig our graves or dig us out of them :
                    or a plank on which we drift to sea ::

will the *we* have gained force enough to shift trade winds ::

                    will we have become capable of concretizing
                    the *we*'s abstraction: of deifying adhesion ::

or will it have required something of us that *we* were not willing to give :

that *I*, each, was not willing to give ::

)

a disappearance, a nest of snakebites—a gluttony muffling the aquifers—borderless, these conspiracies of inflammation—

is *we* a miracle
                or windblown, tenuous, as snow given over to open air,
                                                displaced from the forest's sanctuary

what is its role in this poem
                who or what its point of reference

wicked annunciations, polymers—varnishing our uteri with sticky threnody—& what Gehenna for Prospera & Vattenfall?—

we shuttle between urgencies
                assimilate to crisis
what to do but eat the meat
                off the short ribs of a waning crescent, spit
luster out like sunflower hull

my mother tongue: cuckoo bird. my nation: glamorous cannibal

though the possessive implies a necessary separation from the entity
& not an assemblage of *I* & many like-*I*s

    adrift in daily pageantries: omnipotent alarm clocks, repose reframed as backlit
        pointillism
    as we kneel on the grounds of diversion, rise, argue the relative weights & volumes
    of evil, elect, capitulate, rail & resign & forget, let the exhaustions without balm

reclaim us, we chronic insomniacs, blue-light imbued, flown
over, our sedans scuttling like minnows through early fog

    to work; the route shifts; loans due; local landlords wringing rent. trying to set a little
        back
    when possible. rarely. for emergencies

                    (when pandemic petit mal pirated you
              to the ER, sister, dungeoned your spirit in still waters,
                      your eyelids a jealousy for dragonflies,
                    you were seven days from losing insurance)

this hollowed shibari of american life

ministry of hernia, ministry of bone spur—inheritance of verb on which sun never set—
succession to splinter at horizon, refashion in pyrolysis—

fewer dragonflies, now, than in the once I was raised in. that once more bewildered than my
tongue's subjunctive is scorned

(

if my language   if my language refused   if I refused my language   contradicted

my language   which indicates   if my language ifed   if my language refused

to indicate   opted, rather, to   anticipate, aspire, surrender to slippage

down the esophagus of sensation   to be eaten alive by what my body has sensed   to make the tongue

a contradiction   if my language ifed   if my language   subjuncted

if demand   if desire   if buoyancy   if unpinnable could be

)

if hopelessness is not natural
who has made it their mission to manufacture it

          & to what end?

*& the fruit of pyrolysis—solid solstice, solid night—medium of passage & design—conqueror
of toxin—the indispensable discipline: neuron & myocyte alike—*

at this precise moment in history—

         which has been arrived at following, first, the
         emancipatory cosmic drumstrike, whose oily ringing
         bloomed density into time, irreverent atom, minor key of
         an immaculate vacuum, the color black, many fires, minor
         & behemoth, each dying from the moment they become,
         & hence ostensibly, as we are, alive; each of whose afterlife is

an end of time, a horizon time cannot cross; planets of gas; planets of rock; planets miracling with water; one such which, following an epoch of bacteria allergic to oxygen, then of oxygen, striding in like an unwarranted messiah; following innumerable empires of moss; would convulse & thunder, erupt with not lava, but, at last, a multiplicity of life; life gestated, labored for, a rapturous irony, irreplaceable even in the context of infinity, in which nothing should be irreplaceable—

is occurring

murder by drone (indirectly). murder by sniper (indirectly). murder by cop's skittish finger, its close-strapped metal hound (indirectly). murder by iron mythos of amaranthine expansion (directly).

murder by corporate climate solution (indirectly). murder by nitrogen plant seized by identity crisis (surreptitiously noxious assist to agrobusiness? inflator of ammunition?). murder less by wildfire infection (indirectly) than by refusal to inconvenience gross domestic product (directly).

murder by conscientiously concocted famine (indirectly). murder by fifty-year flood (indirectly). murder by border guard (indirectly). murder not, as reported, by choleric sea, but by the long blink of our landlocked eyes (indirectly). murder (indirectly) progressed by a purportedly progressive percentage of the daily productions of the bodies through which each of our spirits move. murder (directly) by oligarchs' abyssal appetites

closed fists warping space-time
encomiendaing Congo-Kinshasa
plantationing Kentucky State Penitentiary
West Banking Juárez

this morning in Gaza, this morning in Clayton, the mourning cry *where is my brother's heart?*

—tessitura to breach horizon lines—time zones
paper & accordion—rattles,
the decreed boundary, the wraithlike walls—
in certain tongues, the word
to weep has blood in it—

a canal gouging from *émotion* to *émeute*

rhapsodic, the incendiary apiaries—blazing epoch to graceless grace note—paltrier than
period in an era—already heired by liana, lyannaj

language's vital dialetheia
not quite charmolypi
but the truth & dread
of which novel prophets spoke
what is any epiphany
without the company
of fallow havoc
any vision
without mutiny
any cataract
without ibis divine

advent of lichen—advent of orchid—epiphyte muse of concatenation—

when is the sky red—   —aurora. crepuscule. crepuscule. aurora.

what dove trembles between seasons—what shudders out from cumulonimbus' caesura: the
first conditional of being—name me another mercy—tectonic, jellyfish will reign—

my nation, many-tentacled nautilus.
my nation tantalic in the sense of resistance to corrosion. not corruption, which is
    altogether different.

in my nation, we carbon-balance with the blood
of Black children, we overturn the overturners
of money changers' tables, we rewrite narratives in steel, we rewrite narratives of steel,
feign innocence, stick silencers to the assassinating gun, bleach screams into seagull arias
my nation knows what it is doing with language

I a unit of measurement
in the imperial system,

I a small blade
to winnow

lyric to swooning
twig, *I* treacherously

monosyllabic, self-
contained, serpent

twitching in its
own elegant

heart in the heart of a

(hyper-funded police state)
(red scare legacy)
(technocratic looting)
(country I was razed in?
raised in? feasted on?
fattened in?)

seven years between totalities—eight months between trumpeters—as children, we knew to
claim such honey for our tongues—

paradox of the native tongue—   —to know nothing of the structure &
                                                         function of one's own language
                                                         until learned through another's

coronas a rebalancing equation—within that dark, a disinheritance—antithesis to accepted
order—how it quickens the body's meridians

my nation: metastasizing
                              ossuary
my nation: quietly
                      friable in gunpowder mask
my nation: fearless as fools of
                      leaking massacre into the heart of God

                                                         how to be dangerous to
my nation: hands troubling its obdurate waters

: a glass to descry mistletoe austerities

: a matchbox rearing towards its flag

: a blade to peel the warp from its language,

scour what radical

revisions might labor,

plant novel violets in the blank of dawn,

a field for dragonflies,

for the ever-sparer lightning bugs, still gracing the hillsides of our memories

for the child still learning her mother's tongue in the refugee tents of a pilfered
territory

for a father pilfered by a carceral state, his name mythed territory

for the catfish dredging the Ohio's plutonium bloat

for the children inhaling poisoned air, the children drinking
poisoned water

for the child Tamir & the child Emmett, for the mother of Emmett,

our American pietà, patron saint of the necessity of witness, blaze against sclerosing heart

for the mother of the mother of the mother of my mother

for my mother, cleansing our home with the smoking twigs of the juniper

tree abstracted by summer storm

(after her mother, her mother's mother, who did the same with a plant whose name no one

remembers—whose name is only memory's—)

for the tempest, who initiates us to the art of teeth,

amplifying each heat—may she be permitted rest

for Hawai'i & Ayiti & Puerto Rico & Turtle Island &

for Aaron, reproaching pharaoh with a speech of flame

for the betrayers of reticence, fear's apostates, defectors of philosophies of ennui

for Hind Hall's keepers & the Ferguson brave, for the saints of Standing Rock, Tortuguita

who met the forests' holy

for the Mayfield Ten, bulldozing borders with bodies illicit

for the body, mistranslated, the body weighed & appraised illicit

for the land—for the radicle it nurtures—

the posterity mineral imagines, knowing it true—for the imagining,

its diagenesis—its paradox, solid as mineral—for the devotion

that rivers between aspens—for every hair on the aspens' roots,
whose native tongue is sustenance—is *we*—for the deliverance of we—for, even, the *I* I am
(—I cannot abandon it—so must decide what it will carry on its back, jutting forth
like two hands in prayer—), leaning also against your *you*, which leans
against me—

a field, as the physicist's, unified—as the ecologist's, interwoven bodily, elementally,
atomically—as the mystic's, fatidic, designed through its own speaking—as the artist's, an
ecstasy necessarily envisioned before vivified

altar of season, altar of cycle, altar whose touch will assuage the floods
altar of bobcat & the attentive ear, altar of freshwater,
altar of home, bluegrass, blue heron, blue chugging heart where this land's arteries
rendezvous & wed
altar whose cloth is crocheted by my grandmother's hands, half-paralyzed by
corporation—o tenacious love
altar of my body—yes, my body!—altar of this altar we build with our bodies
altar of the aging dogwood, whose body dares itself a question mark
altar of night jasmine—psalm of ambrosia, flare in sightlessness
altar of cultivated agglutination, precipitate gathering in the well of the crucible
altar where I have looked at you & seen my wound & remembered how to bandage it
altar where the *aprézan* blooms, a possibility, an iris rising teal & titanic from calamity's
swamps
altar on which a nation's dust is transmuted back to dust, a future order's fable
altar of metaphor, this oracle whose temple houses our kinships & asymmetries alike
altar of the coexistence of our particulars
altar anointed with the essence of an unknown herb, impatient & nameless, belonging
to no single tongue—its medicine: not apocalypse, but alchemy
& its scent, sweet & staggering as jazz
in this young century's vertiginous heat

Ecclesiastes: Mapleseed

a burial, a kind of birth.

if twice-digested, we absorb the eagle's wings.

our heart beasts. our heart a behemoth
in waiting. our heart & its pinions,
an accurate seraph.

who can say what dark epiphanies
rack the minds of field mice. or any being
so near to earth it can survive
its speech, awful as the ark of the covenant.

we, too, a concentrate of gnostic mysteries.
slight birds. flocking. & patient shifter of stone.

someday, we'll know that even a warcloud
is only water. learning to drink, death

dies in us. learning ascension,
we confound the skein
of centuries, fold power

& verb at our root.
every colossus

we yearn
to become—

we become it.

Acknowledgments

It seems almost impossible to limit the constellation of people who have walked with me throughout this journey to the span of a few short pages. This work exists only because, from my youngest years, I have had my family, friends, teachers, and community rooting for me and illuminating the way. In an attempt to express the inexpressible, I extend my heart:

To my beloved parents, who not only nurtured my love of language from birth but also never discouraged me from pursuing it; my grandmother, whose story-telling was my first introduction to creative writing; my grandfather, whose colorful expressions continually teach me the poetry of our speech; my ever-encouraging cousins; and my little sister, for always (always) keeping me humble—maybe one of these days, I'll take your advice and churn out some hyper-lucrative werewolf smut instead.

To my irreplaceable friends: Zidong, Nancy, Sasha, Austin, Akshay—Brooklyn became a home to me only because I was lucky enough to share it with you. Jeff, Bri, Marc, May—you remind me that friendship, when tended, will find its way across years and borders.

To Carrie, Alison, and Cecilia, for teaching young me the alchemy of a writing community during my first round of Paris years; to Kaila and Chris, for filling those years—and ever after—with your vibrancy and love.

To the Cave Canem Chapbook Prize readers, judge Danez Smith, and P. Scott Cunningham and the entire O, Miami team, for being some of the first people to believe in my work, inspiring me to have confidence in the value of my words, and bestowing upon my scattered documents a beautiful physical body.

To my instructors at the Kentucky Governor's School for the Arts, for being the first to bring poetry into my life; and my instructors at Paducah Public Schools, Vanderbilt University, and New York University, for cultivating me as a young writer and giving me spaces to explore, challenge myself, and grow.

To Maria, for reflecting with me about words and nature beneath the trees of

Green-Wood Cemetery, as well as for the faith you held in my work and your indispensable part in this book's existence.

To my editor, Allie Merola, her assistant, Sonia Gadre, and the magnificent team at Penguin Books, for your generous appreciation of these poems, your attentiveness to their purpose and construction, and the care with which you've looked over every word fragment, stanza break, and ampersand.

To (in no particular order) the Rona Jaffe Foundation, Poetry Foundation and the Ruth Lilly and Dorothy Sargent Rosenberg Fellowship, Tin House, Tupelo Press, Bucknell University, and the New York Foundation for the Arts, for granting me opportunities to study and expand my craft, often bringing within my reach what otherwise would have been inaccessible. Additionally, given how much translating has taught me about my own writing, my gratitude, as well, to the American Literary Translators Association's Emerging Translator Mentorship Program, and especially to my incredible mentor Bill Johnston for teaching me the importance of intentionality, specificity, and attention.

Finally, I am immensely grateful to all of the editors, readers, and publication teams that have so kindly supported my writing along the way. Regarding the poems in this collection, I would like to extend my thanks to:

Prairie Schooner: "Spring in the Key of Pyrocene" and "Ecclesiastes: Mapleseed"

Spoon River Poetry Review: "Thirteen Ways of Looking at a Dead Fish"

Beloit Poetry Journal: "Diaspora Poetica"

Gulf Coast: "Ecclesiastes: Deciduous"

Southern Humanities Review: "Second Parable for the Apocalypse We Built: The Forum"

Quarterly West: "Twister Tri-State"

Academy of American Poets Poem-a-Day: "Ecclesiastes: Thirteen-Year Cicada" and "Singularity"

Narrative: "Lot's Wife" and "Broke-Down Litany for an Empire's End"

Poetry magazine: "If we had known," "Black Girl Kintsugi," "Notes Left for the Ohio River to Read After It Tells Me It Has Forgotten Its Source," "Memory of Mammoth Cave, Provoked by a Pelvic Ultrasound," and "Wild Grasses"

Muzzle Magazine: "Ecclesiastes: New Madrid Fault"

Rattle: "Katabasis"

Southeast Review: "Elegy for the Living"

Great River Review: "Parable for the Apocalypse We Built, ii: Doe of the Haruspex"

Nimrod International Journal: "Demeter & Child"

New South: "Parable for the Apocalypse We Built" and "Union"

Glass: A Journal of Poetry: "Psalm for the Unloved Body"

Frontier Poetry: "Antigone in the Bluegrass"

Sundog Lit: "Notes on What I've Heard Called the End of America" (portions of which became "Broke-Down Litany for an Empire's End")

With love and love and love,
Marissa

Notes

The italicized portions of "Antigone in the Bluegrass" are taken, with some minor alterations, from Aída Chávez's article "Louisville Police Left the Body of David McAtee on the Street for 12 Hours," published on June 1, 2020, in *The Intercept*.

"Twister Tristate" was inspired by the November 15, 2005, tornado outbreak, which affected several areas of the Midwest and mid-South.

"If we had known," takes as its theme the January 2009 ice storm, which affected a large swath of the southeastern United States. It placed Kentucky under a state of emergency, with my region in the far west of the state being the worst impacted. Besides the damage done to homes and infrastructure by fallen trees and the ice itself, some areas were also left without electricity for weeks.

The form of "Parable for the Apocalypse We Built: The Forum" is modeled after C. P. Cavafy's poem "Waiting for the Barbarians."

"Thirteen Ways of Looking at a Dead Fish" was inspired by the February 2023 train derailment disaster in East Palestine, Ohio, as well as the 1999 reveal of radioactive contaminants from a uranium enrichment plant in Paducah, Kentucky. Material for this poem was sourced from articles in *The Washington Post*, *Willamette Week*, *Yahoo! News*, WFMJ.com, and other outlets. The italicized tenth section draws its language from Joby Warrick's 1999 *Washington Post* exposé "In Harm's Way, and in the Dark: Workers Exposed to Plutonium at U.S. Plant."

Portions of "Broke-Down Litany for an Empire's End" reference the novel *Rebecca* by Daphne du Maurier.

"For Columbia" was written after the violent sweeping of Columbia's and City College's Gaza solidarity encampments by NYPD in the spring of 2024, during which time I was an adjunct professor at Columbia's women's college, Barnard. That morning, students had occupied Hamilton Hall, renaming it Hind's Hall after the young Palestinian girl murdered, along with her rescuers, by Israel, after days of being trapped in a car with the corpses of her family members. Columbia's encampment was the most visible of a nationwide wave of student movements aimed at spurring universities to divest from the genocide, almost all of which met similar repression.

The form of "Black Girl Kintsugi" is inspired by the Japanese art of kintsugi, in which gold- or silver-dusted lacquer is used to repair broken pottery.

"Singularity" is inspired by the poem of the same name by Marie Howe.

"The Living Soil" shares its title with the seminal book on organic farming by Eve Balfour, known as the mother of the organic agricultural movement. The poem incorporates subheadings from her table of contents into its material. Notably, Eve Balfour is the niece of British politician Arthur Balfour, whose 1917 Balfour Declaration pledged Britain's support of the Zionist colonization of Palestinian lands. The poem's line "best endeavours to facilitate the achievement of [the ally's] object" is a quote taken from this Declaration.

"Altar-Mondialism" features language inspired by or drawn from several poets. "I have looked at you & seen my wound" is written after a line by Dionne Brand; "truth & dread" is a reference to Adrienne Rich; "coexistence of our particulars" comes from Aimé Césaire; and Patrick Chamoiseau's and Édouard Glissant's cowritten book *Manifestos* offers "aprézan" and "lyannaj" to the poem's lexicon. I'll end this book with *Manifestos*'s words of defiant hope in troubled times: "In every crisis, right from the start, there is a now that opens—an aprézan."

MARISSA DAVIS is a poet and translator from Paducah, Kentucky. Her writing has appeared in *Poetry* magazine, *Narrative*, *Gulf Coast*, and *Prairie Schooner*, among other journals. Her chapbook, *My Name & Other Languages I Am Learning How to Speak* (Jai-Alai Books, 2020) was selected for Cave Canem's 2019 Toi Derricotte and Cornelius Eady Chapbook Prize. Davis holds an MFA from New York University and was a 2024 Ruth Lilly and Dorothy Sargent Rosenberg Fellow. Following years in Nashville, Tennessee, and Brooklyn, New York, she now lives in Paris, France, where she is pursuing a master's in Editorial, Economic, and Technical Translation at the Sorbonne Nouvelle.

GAROUS ABDOLMALEKIAN
Lean Against This Late Hour

PAIGE ACKERSON-KIELY
Dolefully, A Rampart Stands

JOHN ASHBERY
Selected Poems
Self-Portrait in a Convex Mirror

PAUL BEATTY
Joker, Joker, Deuce

JOSHUA BENNETT
Owed
The Sobbing School
The Study of Human Life

TED BERRIGAN
The Sonnets

LAUREN BERRY
The Lifting Dress

JOE BONOMO
Installations

PHILIP BOOTH
Lifelines: Selected Poems
 1950–1999
Selves

JIM CARROLL
Fear of Dreaming:
 The Selected Poems
Living at the Movies
Void of Course

SU CHO
The Symmetry of Fish

ADRIENNE CHUNG
Organs of Little Importance

RIO CORTEZ
Golden Ax

MARISSA DAVIS
End of Empire

ALISON HAWTHORNE DEMING
Genius Loci
Rope
Stairway to Heaven

CARL DENNIS
Another Reason
Callings
Earthborn
New and Selected Poems
 1974–2004
Night School
Practical Gods
Ranking the Wishes
Unknown Friends

DIANE DI PRIMA
Loba

STUART DISCHELL
Backwards Days
Dig Safe

STEPHEN DOBYNS
Velocities: New and Selected
 Poems 1966–1992

EDWARD DORN
Way More West

HEID E. ERDRICH
Little Big Bully

ROGER FANNING
The Middle Ages

ADAM FOULDS
The Broken Word: An Epic
 Poem of the British Empire
 in Kenya, and the Mau Mau
 Uprising Against It

CARRIE FOUNTAIN
Burn Lake
Instant Winner
The Life

AMY GERSTLER
Dearest Creature
Ghost Girl
Index of Women
Is This My Final Form?
Medicine
Nerve Storm
Scattered at Sea

EUGENE GLORIA
Drivers at the Short-Time Motel
Hoodlum Birds
My Favorite Warlord
Sightseer in This Killing City

DEBORA GREGER
In Darwin's Room

ZEINA HASHEM BECK
O

TERRANCE HAYES
American Sonnets for My Past
 and Future Assassin
Hip Logic
How to Be Drawn
Lighthead
So to Speak
Wind in a Box

NATHAN HOKS
The Narrow Circle

ROBERT HUNTER
Sentinel and Other Poems

MARY KARR
Viper Rum

W. B. KECKLER
Sanskrit of the Body

JACK KEROUAC
Book of Blues
Book of Haikus
Book of Sketches

JOANNA KLINK
Circadian
Excerpts from a
 Secret Prophecy
The Nightfields
Raptus

JOANNE KYGER
As Ever: Selected Poems

ANN LAUTERBACH
Door
Hum
If in Time: Selected Poems
 1975–2000
On a Stair
Or to Begin Again
Spell
Under the Sign

CORINNE LEE
Plenty
Pyx

PENGUIN POETS

PHILLIS LEVIN
May Day
Mr. Memory & Other Poems

PATRICIA LOCKWOOD
Motherland Fatherland
  Homelandsexuals

WILLIAM LOGAN
Rift of Light

J. MICHAEL MARTINEZ
Museum of the Americas
Tarta Americana

ADRIAN MATEJKA
The Big Smoke
Map to the Stars
Mixology
Somebody Else Sold the World

AMBER McBRIDE
Thick with Trouble

MICHAEL McCLURE
Huge Dreams: San Francisco
  and Beat Poems

ROSE McLARNEY
Colorfast
Forage
Its Day Being Gone

DAVID MELTZER
David's Copy:
  The Selected Poems of
  David Meltzer

TERESA K. MILLER
Borderline Fortune

ROBERT MORGAN
Dark Energy
Terroir

CAROL MUSKE-DUKES
Blue Rose
An Octave Above Thunder:
  New and Selected Poems
Red Trousseau
Twin Cities

ALICE NOTLEY
Being Reflected Upon
Certain Magical Acts
Culture of One
The Descent of Alette
Disobedience
For the Ride
In the Pines
Mysteries of Small Houses

WILLIE PERDOMO
The Crazy Bunch
The Essential Hits of
  Shorty Bon Bon

DANIEL POPPICK
Fear of Description

LIA PURPURA
It Shouldn't Have Been
  Beautiful

LAWRENCE RAAB
The History of Forgetting
Visible Signs:
  New and Selected Poems

BARBARA RAS
The Last Skin
One Hidden Stuff

M.S. REDCHERRIES
mother

MICHAEL ROBBINS
Alien vs. Predator
The Second Sex
Walkman

PATTIANN ROGERS
Flickering
Generations
Holy Heathen Rhapsody
Quickening Fields
Wayfare

SAM SAX
Madness

ROBYN SCHIFF
Information Desk: An Epic
A Woman of Property

WILLIAM STOBB
Absentia
Nervous Systems

TRYFON TOLIDES
An Almost Pure Empty Walking

VINCENT TORO
Hivestruck
Tertulia

PAUL TRAN
All the Flowers Kneeling

SARAH VAP
Viability

ANNE WALDMAN
Gossamurmur
Kill or Cure
Manatee/Humanity
Mesopotopia
Trickster Feminism

JAMES WELCH
Riding the Earthboy 40

PHILIP WHALEN
Overtime: Selected Poems

PHILLIP B. WILLIAMS
Mutiny

MIA S. WILLIS
the space between men

ROBERT WRIGLEY
Anatomy of Melancholy and
  Other Poems
Beautiful Country
Box
Earthly Meditations:
  New and Selected Poems
Lives of the Animals
Reign of Snakes
The True Account of Myself
  as a Bird

MARK YAKICH
The Importance of Peeling
  Potatoes in Ukraine
Spiritual Exercises
Unrelated Individuals Forming
  a Group Waiting to Cross